## This Journal Belongs to:

_____

_____

_____

# TAMING THE MONSTER

## JOURNAL

---

Based on
*It Came from Within!*
by Andy Stanley

Multnomah Publishers® *Sisters, Oregon*

TAMING THE MONSTER
published by Multnomah Publishers, Inc.
© 2006 by Andy Stanley
International Standard Book Number: 1-59052-651-1

Cover design by DesignWorks Group, Inc.
Interior design and typeset by Katherine Lloyd, The DESK

Unless otherwise indicated, Scripture quotations are from:
*The Holy Bible,* New International Version © 1973, 1984 by International Bible Society,
used by permission of Zondervan Publishing House.

Other Scripture quotations are from:
*The Holy Bible,* English Standard Version (ESV) © 2001
by Crossway Bibles, a division of Good News Publishers.
Used by permission. All rights reserved.
*New American Standard Bible®* (NASB) © 1960, 1977, 1995
by the Lockman Foundation. Used by permission.

*Multnomah* is a trademark of Multnomah Publishers, Inc.,
and is registered in the U.S. Patent and Trademark Office.
The colophon is a trademark of Multnomah Publishers, Inc.

Printed in the United States of America

For information:
MULTNOMAH PUBLISHERS, INC.
601 N LARCH STREET
SISTERS, OREGON 97759

06 07 08 09 10 11—10 9 8 7 6 5 4 3 2 1 0

*The heart is deceitful above all things,*
*and desperately sick; who can understand it?*

JEREMIAH 17:9, ESV

**Dr. Morbius: My evil self is at the door, and I have no power to stop it!**

FORBIDDEN PLANET (1956)

*Eventually your heart—the real you—will outpace your attempts*
*to monitor and modify everything you say and do.*
*The unresolved issues stirring around undetected in your heart*
*will eventually work their way to the surface.*

IT CAME FROM WITHIN!

*Watch over your heart with all diligence,*
*For from it flow the springs of life.*

PROVERBS 4:23 (NASB)

*If you don't like the fruit that keeps cluttering up
your backyard, the only real solution is to dig up the tree by
the roots and alleviate the issue once and for all. If you
deal with the source, you have dealt with the problem.*

IT CAME FROM WITHIN!

General: When an armed and threatening power lands uninvited in our capitol, we don't meet him with tea and cookies!

EARTH VS. THE FLYING SAUCERS (1956)

*If it suddenly became impossible for us to cover up all the junk we normally hide from the rest of humanity, I have a feeling we would all get real motivated to deal with the condition of our hearts.*

It Came from Within!

**Dr. Jekyll: Gentlemen like me have to be very careful of what we do or say.**

Dr. Jekyll and Mr. Hyde (1931)

*"But the things that come out of the mouth come from the heart,
and these make a man 'unclean.'"*

MATTHEW 15:18

What's in your heart comes out at home, where you've
turned off the "safety" and let down your defenses.
That's when the heart exposes itself in the most negative
ways to the people you love the most.

IT CAME FROM WITHIN!

Newt: My mommy always said there were
no monsters—no real ones. But there are,
aren't there?

Ripley: Yes, there are.

Newt: Why do they tell little kids that?

Ripley: Most of the time it's true.

ALIENS (1986)

Guilt, anger, greed, jealousy. These are the four primary enemies of the heart—
four life-blocking agents that become lodged in the heart,
poisoning our relationships, our faith, and our character.
These corrosive forces gain strength from the darkness. Secrecy is their
greatest ally. Left to their own, they grow in power and influence,
like a lab experiment gone terribly wrong.

IT CAME FROM WITHIN!

**Joan: I expected to be frightened**

**on my wedding night, but nothing like this.**

INVASION OF THE SAUCER MEN (1957)

*Guilt, anger, greed, jealousy—all are habit-forming. And like any*
*habit that goes unchecked, over time they come to define us.*
*These disorders become such a part of us that we no longer view them*
*as issues to be resolved. Instead, we dismiss these destructive*
*habits as characteristics hard-wired into our personality.*

It Came from Within!

**Doc: Anywhere in the galaxy**

**this is a nightmare.**

FORBIDDEN PLANET (1956)

_I wish a changed heart was as simple as singing a song or praying a prayer._
_Sometimes it is, but in most cases it's not. It requires effort._
_Sometimes it requires pain. And there's always some discomfort involved._
_A changed heart is the result of forming some new habits—_
_some exercises for the heart._

It Came from Within!

**Miles: I take a dim view**

**of watching my own destruction.**

<small>Invasion of the Body Snatchers (1956)</small>

*Every seasoned vampire slayer knows that a little bit of light is all
one needs to separate the good guys from the dead guys.
Secrets, like the walking undead of gothic horror films,
lose their power when exposed to light.*

It Came from Within!

*And the prayer offered in faith will make the sick person well; the Lord will raise him up. If he has sinned, he will be forgiven. Therefore confess your sins to each other and pray for each other so that you may be healed.*

JAMES 5:15–16

*The truth is, you cannot resolve your differences with God if you are unwilling to resolve your differences with men and women. You cannot be in fellowship with the Father and out of fellowship with others over something you have done.*

It Came from Within!

Jan Compton: Nothing you can be is more terrible than what I am.

THE BRAIN THAT WOULDN'T DIE (1962)

*Christ paid a debt he did not owe and one we could not pay.
That kind of love should motivate us to pay those debts
we can pay to those we do owe.*

IT CAME FROM WITHIN!

*In the shadow of the cross all our excuses, all our griping, all our rationalization amount to nothing. His death was for our good, and his commands regarding confession and reconciliation are for our good as well. Confession enables us to come out from the shadow of sin and into the light where all things are made new.*

IT CAME FROM WITHIN!

Manning: What kind of sin could
a man commit in a single lifetime
to bring this upon himself?

THE AMAZING COLOSSAL MAN (1957)

_Of the four enemies vying for control of our hearts, anger is perhaps the most dangerous._
_When unleashed with unbridled intensity, anger leaves a trail of destruction_
_in its wake. But behind all the huffing and puffing, ranting_
_and raving, brewing and stewing is the most basic of_
_human experiences: We just aren't getting our way._

<small>IT CAME FROM WITHIN!</small>

Steve (voiceover): Tokyo, a smoldering memorial to the unknown, an unknown which at this very moment still prevails and could at any time lash out with its terrible destruction anywhere else in the world.

GODZILLA, KING OF THE MONSTERS (1956)

*Show me an angry person and I'll show you a hurt person.*
*And I guarantee you that person is hurt because*
*something has been taken.*

IT CAME FROM WITHIN!

More times than we care to admit, the shrapnel of our anger
pierces those closest to us, loved ones who are innocent
and clueless as to what caused us to detonate in their presence.

IT CAME FROM WITHIN!

*Be kind and compassionate to one another,*
*forgiving each other, just as in Christ God forgave you.*

EPHESIANS 4:32

*Deal with your anger and you take away the enemy's foothold;*
*refuse to deal with it and you must prepare for the worst.*

IT CAME FROM WITHIN!

**Lt. McPherson:** I wonder if this thing can read minds.

**Eddie:** Well, if it can, it's gonna be real mad when it gets to me.

THE THING FROM ANOTHER WORLD (1951)

*These monsters of the heart cannot withstand the light of exposure.*
*For you to tell your story would be to drag them out into the light.*
*Can you see that by forcing yourself to bring your story to*
*light you may deal your anger a fatal blow?*

IT CAME FROM WITHIN!

**Det. Sgt. Donovan: It's not for man to interfere in the ways of God.**

I Was a Teenage Werewolf (1957)

*How long are you going to allow the people who*
*have hurt you to control your life?*

IT CAME FROM WITHIN!

*Your pain is not a trophy to show off. It is not a story to tell.*
*It is potentially poison to your soul. To refuse to forgive*
*is to choose to self-destruct.*

IT CAME FROM WITHIN!

Klaatu: Your choice is simple. Join us and live in peace or pursue your present course and face obliteration. We shall be waiting for your answer.

The Day the Earth Stood Still (1951)

_Forgiveness runs so contrary to our sense of justice and fairness that it's unlikely
we will ever feel like forgiving. But in the Scriptures forgiveness is
never presented as a feeling; it is always described as a decision.
Forgiveness is a gift we decide to give in spite of how we feel._

IT CAME FROM WITHIN!

*Greed is not a financial issue; it is a heart issue. Financial gain doesn't
make greedy people less greedy. Financial gain or loss doesn't
change anything, because greed emanates from the heart.*

It Came from Within!

*"Watch out! Be on your guard against all kinds of greed;
a man's life does not consist in the abundance of his possessions."*

LUKE 12:15

**The Vicar: Beware! Beware the beast within!**

WALLACE & GROMIT: THE CURSE OF THE WERE-RABBIT (2005)

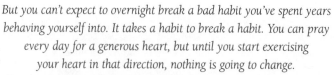

*But you can't expect to overnight break a bad habit you've spent years behaving yourself into. It takes a habit to break a habit. You can pray every day for a generous heart, but until you start exercising your heart in that direction, nothing is going to change.*

IT CAME FROM WITHIN!

Howard: It's hungry! It has to be fed constantly—

or it will reach out its magnetic arm and grab

at anything within its reach and kill it.

It's monstrous, Stewart, monstrous.

It grows bigger and bigger!

THE MAGNETIC MONSTER (1953)

*This is Jesus' definition of a greedy person: a person who stores up things for himself but is not rich toward God. Being "rich toward God" is Jesus-talk for being generous toward those in need. A greedy person is the man or woman who saves carefully but gives sparingly.*

IT CAME FROM WITHIN!

*When I have money, I get rid of it quickly,*
*lest it find a way into my heart.*

JOHN WESLEY

**Maj. Purdue: It's got to kill us or starve,**

**and we've got to kill it or die.**

It! The Terror from Beyond Space (1958)

_You've got to give to the point that it forces you to adjust your lifestyle._
_If you are consuming and saving to the point that there_
_is little or nothing to give, you are greedy._

It Came from Within!

*Iago: O beware, my lord, of jealousy.*
*'Tis the green-eyed monster which doth mock the meat it feeds on.*

OTHELLO (1622)

*Jealousy doesn't register as a grudge we are holding against God.
But that's exactly what it is. The irony, of course, is that the
people we are jealous of can do nothing to remedy the situation.*

IT CAME FROM WITHIN!

*Death and Destruction are never satisfied,*
*and neither are the eyes of man.*

PROVERBS 27:20

---

---

---

---

---

---

---

---

---

---

---

---

---

---

---

---

---

---

---

---

*There will always be someone who is richer, skinnier, more talented, better connected, or just plain luckier than you. And until you find a way to deal with your jealous heart, you will be unable to follow the most basic of all Christian tenets—love one another.*

IT CAME FROM WITHIN!

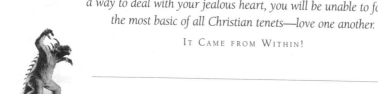

*You want something but don't get it. You kill and covet,*
*but you cannot have what you want.*

JAMES 4:2

_____

_____

_____

_____

_____

_____

_____

_____

_____

_____

_____

_____

_____

_____

_____

_____

_____

_____

_____

_____

_____

_____

*Your real problem isn't with the people whose stuff you envy; it's with your Creator.*
*God owes you, and you're holding a grudge against Him. And until you*
*face up to this simple but oh so convicting truth, jealousy will*
*continue to terrorize your life and wreak havoc in your relationships.*

IT CAME FROM WITHIN!

Major Cartwright: The trouble with these scientific types is they can't see the easy way out of anything. It's got to be complicated if it's going to work.

X THE UNKNOWN (1956)

_____

_____

_____

_____

_____

_____

_____

_____

_____

_____

_____

_____

_____

_____

_____

_____

*You have been invited to bring every frustration and fear to God.*
*There is nothing too big, nothing too small. You bring 'em all.*
*If it's important to you then it's important to God.*
*Because you are important to God.*

IT CAME FROM WITHIN!

*Every good and perfect gift is from above, coming down from
the Father of the heavenly lights, who does not change like shifting shadows.*

JAMES 1:17

*Our kids share more than our physical genes. They may also share our propensities towards anger, guilt, greed, and jealousy. Our children are among the primary reasons we need to tackle these issues head-on in our own lives.*

IT CAME FROM WITHIN!

Sometimes I wish I were a little kid again.
Skinned knees are easier to fix than broken hearts.

AUTHOR UNKNOWN

*The question I must wrestle with as a parent is, "When my kids pack their cars and leave home once and for all, what will be packed away in their hearts? And what can I do now to prepare them for the day when their hearts are totally their responsibility?"*

IT CAME FROM WITHIN!

**Kurt: The paths of experimentation twist and turn through mountains of miscalculations and often lose themselves in error and darkness!**

THE BRAIN THAT WOULDN'T DIE (1962)

*Nothing destroys an individual's capacity for intimacy like sexual impurity. So Satan leverages our anger for his own ends, and in the end, we pay. Dearly.*

IT CAME FROM WITHIN!

*Anger, greed, guilt, and jealousy are the antithesis of love. As long as these four monsters grow unchecked in your heart, your efforts to love will be short-lived, thwarted.*
*No amount of effort on your part can compensate. The purest of motives will not prevail. You cannot love while harboring one or more of these enemies.*

IT CAME FROM WITHIN!

The Monitor: It is indeed typical that you Earth people refuse to believe in the superiority of any world but your own. Children looking into a magnifying glass, imagining the image you see is the image of your true size.

Dr. Meacham: Our true size is the size of our God!

THIS ISLAND EARTH (1955)

*Like a doctor whose skilled hands poke and probe until they find a sensitive spot,
so God's truth has a way of finding its mark. But none of that
can happen until you give God access to those sensitive,
otherwise off-limits areas of your life.*

<small>IT CAME FROM WITHIN!</small>

Klaatu: I won't resort to threats, Mr. Harley.

I merely tell you the future of your planet

is at stake.

The Day the Earth Stood Still (1951)

*Confess, forgive, give, celebrate. These four habits change everything because they free us to express and experience the most powerful force the human soul has ever encountered: unconditional love.*

Lt. Ray Makonnen: You know, Captain, every year of my life I grow more and more convinced that the wisest and the best is to fix our attention on the good and the beautiful. If you just take the time to look at it.

THE PHANTOM PLANET (1961)

Mourn not for us, for we have known the light,

Have looked on beauty, have lived in peace and love.

Grieve but for those who go alone, unwise,

To die in darkness, never having seen the Sun.

"THE STAR," THE TWILIGHT ZONE (1985)